Praise for Esther Davis-Thompson's MotherLove

"An empowering collection of reflections, quotations and affirmations."—*EBONY*

"This book is a treasure-trove."
—*Lucia Herndon, Columnist, THE PHILADELPHIA INQUIRER*

"Impressive . . . *MotherLove* reminds us we are our best thing."—*NIKKI GIOVANNI, poet*

"Beautifully lyrical reflections on motherhood in the African American community."
—*PUBLISHERS WEEKLY*

"Personal, inspiring, empowering, and timely. Building on the commitment of African American women to institute positive change, *MotherLove* feeds the spirit of the African American community's march forward into a new millenium.".
—*FEMINIST BOOKSTORE NEWS*

"Powerful and nurturing."
—*Barnett Wright, PHILADELPHIA TRIBUNE*

"Rich with affirmation, common sense, and wisdom about recovering one's spiritual 'motherspace' . . . a gift to women trying to mother well."
—*THE OTHER SIDE*

"An empowering compilation that feed[s] the spirit and nourish[es] the soul."
—*BLACK ISSUES BOOK REVIEW*

Raising Up Queens

Also by Esther Davis-Thompson

MotherLove:
Reinventing a Good and Blessed Future
for Our Children

Raising Up Queens

Loving Our Daughters Loud and Strong

by Esther Davis-Thompson

Innisfree
Press, Inc.

A call to the
deep heart's core

Published by
Innisfree Press, Inc.
136 Roumfort Road
Philadelphia, PA 19119-1632
VISIT OUR WEB SITE AT WWW.INNISFREEPRESS.COM

Cover artwork © 2000 by Kimberly Camp.
"Our Women Keep Our Skies from Falling, II"

Cover design by Hugh Duffy, PhD Design, Carneys Point, NJ

Original graphics by Indira Johnson
© Shanti Foundation for Peace
Reprinted by special arrangement
with the Shanti Foundation for Peace.

Library of Congress Cataloging-in-Publication Data
Davis-Thompson, Esther, (date).
Raising up queens : loving our daughters loud and strong /
by Esther Davis-Thompson.
ISBN 1-880913-46-1
1. Mothers and daughters—United States. 2. Afro-
American mothers—Psychology. 3. Afro-American
girls—Psychology. 4. Afro-American mothers—Prayer-
books and devotions—English. 5. Child rearing—Religious
aspects. 6. Afro-American women—Psychology. I. Title.
HQ755.85.D39   2000
306.874'3—dc21
00-026798

The quotation from Maya Angelou's inaugural poem,
ON THE PULSE OF MORNING,
copyright © 1993 by Maya Angelou,
is reprinted by permission of Random House, Inc.

For my mother,

Ruth

and

For my daughters,

Amanda

Sarah

Colleen

Ashley

FRANKFORD

FRANKFORD

"Lift up your faces, you have a piercing need
For this bright morning dawning for you."

—Maya Angelou
ON THE PULSE OF MORNING

Contents

Gratitudes

I had a woman-centered childhood. All around me the most beautiful Real Women swarmed and fussed and tended and cleaned and sewed and did hair and talked and laughed and cried and prayed and sang. And all of my adult life I have tried to figure out how they grew to be as wonderful as they were. Somehow these women took the essence of the raw experiences that life handed them and spun it into enough golden rope to pull up the children. And my secret prayer has always been to be as Strong, as Proud, as Loving, Capable, Orderly, Calm, and Real and Resilient and Beautiful and Present and Powerful as they.

These exquisite women were my Queen examples. My examples of how to be and how not to be. These women took my hands and pulled me up up up to an awareness that if I couldn't do anything else in this life I'd just better believe. Believe. Believe that God is really there/here. Believe that I am accountable, not only to God, but to every living soul who ever crosses my path or looks my way. Believe there will always be a good meal. A clean, warm place to eat and talk and sleep. An honest way to make a living. A noble way to give out Love. A way back from Trouble. A way for Good to happen.

Refusing to believe for Good was the major sin.

And so in writing this book, I wish to express my gratitude to some of these Queens of Spirit: my mother, Ruth; my aunt Althea Turner; my church mother Lottie Miller. And I wish to honor the spirits of those who have crossed over: my great-grandmother Mary Ruth Habersham, my grandmother Dorothy Virginia Davis, and my church mother Anna B. Blocker. Thank you for loving me more than enough.

To my circle of loved ones—my husband, Art (who still puts up with my computer crises) and my children Art Jr, James, Shawn, Patrick, Amanda, Sarah, Colleen, Ryan, Ashley, Alex, who have patiently walked me through the writing of this book, allowing my frequent pre-occupation to intrude on their lives—I am not ignorant of the sacrifices. I am grateful. And to my new daughter-friends Jeanette, Janet (Mookie), and Sibongile, and my incredibly delightful grandson Little James (my newest sweet inspiration), my sister-friends Jem, Cordella, Gloria, Yolanda, Eileen, Kemba, Norma, Loyce, and Barbara, my mother, Ruth, and my sisters, Van and Josie, thank you for always listening, always encouraging, always reading, always validating, always supporting and always inspiring.

To Marcia Broucek, publisher at Innisfree Press, *the* most intuitive editor, patient guidance counselor and friend, listener and encourager . . . thank you.

And as always . . . I thank God, whose Grace truly is always sufficient. Much, much gratitude for the many, many Blessings.

Raising Up Queens

It is time . . .

It is time for a renewed passion about our Woman-Work.

If we want our daughters to grow up toward the Highest end of themselves—to walk in abundance, to walk in self-confidence, to be free enough to have good relationships, to be well-prepared to love and nurture their own children—we have to be willing to examine our own lives. To examine the place inside us where our own woman-notions have settled and developed us into who we are. To ask ourselves if these beliefs are still valid. Still in our best interest. Still solid enough to support ourselves and our daughters. We must ask ourselves if our beliefs are reflecting the voice of divine protection, guidance, and direction that God has gifted to us.

Although we have, at times, been a very visible cornerstone of the African American community, we have at other times gone through great pains to hide the Real Self that we are—body, soul, spirit—and to masquerade as the image we felt we were allowed to be.

As we look back at the strengths and power of the women who walked before us, we are able to see just how much their press forward depended upon their willingness to love themselves and their men and their children, unconditionally, as precious creations of God. We are able to see how far their belief in their entitlement to their Good carried them. If the Queen-women who walked before us had not loved themselves and believed in themselves, they couldn't have survived. If they hadn't trusted the voice of God, as spoken through their feminine spirits . . . instructing them to pass their powerful ways of loving, their ways of hearing Spirit, on to their daughters so that the loving could keep happening and the Spirit could keep being heard . . . their children would not have survived.

How else could we have gotten to Love from the experiences of slave mothers who were smacked so very hard by life, except their Real Love was carried on God-breath down through the generations of women? And how else could we have come to know such Strength as theirs were it not for their Real Love that tempered the strong winds of adversity, driving their own good seed-Strengths firmly into our generation of women?

The history of the Queen-women who walked before us taught us to protect others . . . sometimes at the steep cost of neglecting self. For our men, for our children, we have been the quiet strength, the burden-bearers, the nurturers, the joy, the peace, the love, the hope, the courage, the backseat drivers, the overt and the hidden power, the rescuers, the reconcilers, the fixers, the healers, the treasure chest and the treasure, the abode and often the ones who had to build the abode.

Our experiences have taught us to conceal our most tender feelings to keep them from being trampled upon. And so we have also, as times dictated, been the angry ones, the ashamed ones, the guilt-ridden ones, the tired ones, the oppressed ones, the sorry ones, the saddest ones, the strangest ones.

Our intuition has taught us to keep our spirits—our most treasured part of self—high up on a shelf away from transgressors, away from those who would force us to change against our will, away from those who did not have our best interests at heart, away from those who could destroy us with an action or a look or a word. Who we have been has, for a long time now, depended entirely on who someone else needed us to be. The dreams in our hearts haven't always mattered. The thoughts in our minds haven't always counted for much. But today is a new day.

There is a time when it is our Woman-Work to bend and bend and bend. Give and give and give of ourselves. Understand and understand others. Accept, accept, accept circumstances. Stand still and upright and strong so others can lean against you and grow their own strength. Clean up and clean up. Cook and cook. Help and help and help and help.

But there is a time, too, when it is our Woman-Work to stop and listen to our lives. Listen to the sounds of spirit our lives are emitting. Listen to hear if there is enough of Love. Listen to hear if there is enough of God. Listen to hear if there is enough real power to facilitate moving ourselves and our daughters forward toward our High Places of Good.

Could it be that God is calling us back from a bout of self-abandonment to know and listen to ourselves again? Could it be that the only way we will be able to guide our daughters to the next level of the High Road is to walk up there ourselves?

Could it really be time to just stop and listen to what the Inner Woman has been trying to tell us?

Could it really be time to surrender our pain so we can go out seeking more joy?

Could it be that it is our major task, as mothers of daughters, to pass the mantle of God-awareness and Real Love-awareness on to our daughters? Entrusting these new women to carry their God-Breath further into the generations, using their willingness to believe what we teach them and the strength we seed into them?

Clothing ourselves in new hope and new faith and in new strength and new love. Gathering up our spirits for a revival with our Creator. Stepping over our own bodies mortified by tiredness. Jumping over rivers of our own murky fear. Leaping from one mountaintop of new faith to another to avoid the pitfalls of self-doubt, self-pity, and self-effacement. Making, for ourselves, a lovely Queen-crown of High Thoughts to wear as we walk wherever.

Could it be that this is the only way we will get to meet our daughters on the good road of peace and abundant life?

Once there was a girl . . .

Once there was a girl . . .

Once there was a girl
who wanted to be a Queen
because she wanted to live her life
in High and Beautiful Places.

Once there was a girl
who wanted to be a mother,
so bad
because she thought all mothers were Queens.
They all seemed to smell so sweet.
And smile so pretty and act so real.

Really, a Queen-Mother is what she wanted to be.
To rule over her life and her people
and feed them
and play with them
and sing them to sleep at night.

Once there was a woman
who wanted to be a Mother-Queen
and what I want to know is . . .
is she going to die trying?

From Pain to Healing

Can we talk? . . .

So many of us are struggling with the basic issues of motherhood, having a hard time making it . . . having a hard time loving our daughters strong. Probably because it feels like no one is loving us. Love has become so alien to some of us that hope seems like a hazard and loving seems like a risky thing to do, even for our children.

Here we come hobbling to you, Lord. Some of us are dragging our hearts. Some of us can barely lift our heads. Many of us are devoid of hope. Many of us have tried an inordinate amount of times, tried and tried and tried, and we're about ready to quit.

We're coming from destructive marriages. We're coming with black eyes and bruised emotions. We're coming with anger that we've had for so long it seems like a best friend. And we're coming for the answers before we have to see ourselves mirrored in our daughter's tears and in their confusion, in their mis-steps and in their terror.

Today, Lord, can we talk about the woundedness of women? The woundedness that keeps us walking our Low Places when we've really been wanting to walk up in the High Places of our lives.

How long? . . .

. . . Yes, Lord, I heard you. I heard you the first time . . . but I couldn't stop myself. How does a woman stop being a ball of pain if a ball of pain is all she knows to be? How does a woman stop being a punching bag? How does a woman stop choosing bad relationships? How does a woman stop giving over her power? How does a woman stop walking out a life of pain if pain is what she knows best and she doesn't even know how or why or even when, for sure, she started knowing pain? Pain is what you learn to be when pain is your familiar.

How long have we known this inner shattering? Since Eve? This peculiar cringing of emotions that creates craters in our self-image, afflicts our reasoning, and causes our hope to evaporate.

And . . . how long have we had to learn to re-remember faith after a long bout of impatience? Since Sarah?

So many of us are broken, and we've come to realize that we're broken . . . but how DO we become whole?

Will you tell me how we can raise ourselves up from our hard places, our low places, our nauseatingly ugly places, to walk in the High Place of the best that we are, the most real that we are, the most Royal and Divine that we are?

. . . what if I sit here? Will you talk to me? Will you smell our pain with me?

Could you tell me? . . .

So many of our daughters are frightened because they know something of our woundedness, but little about our Faith. They know more of the wounds of their mothers and their grandmothers than they do of the Faithfulness of God. Somehow the wounds keep over-shadowing it all.

Could you tell me if there is some way we can raise our daughters through all this pain, through all this frightfulness, through all this uncertainty, through all this heaviness, right back up to you?

Who's going to teach our new daughter-women to love the children strong if we who are women now don't come back from this treacherous journey we're on and get back onto our path to our High Places?

Who will pass on the ways of women loving strong, if we are so wounded that we can only pass on our wounds?

. . . what if I sit very quiet and still? Do you think you could tell me the secrets you locked into the cells of my spirit, that sing so high-pitched I can barely hear . . . yet?

Learning pain . . .

Perhaps you grew up seeing your mother . . . or your aunt, your grandmother, your neighbor-women . . . experiencing that brand of emotional pain that comes from being wounded by the words, the actions, the hands of those who were supposed to love them the most? And now, years later, do they still wear the look of a woman who got beat up last night for no good reason? Do they still walk a few steps behind? Do you still see them crying invisible tears?

If you were raised through the humiliation of your mother's pain, you probably watched her learn not to cry when hurt, learn how to stiffen herself against blows . . . maybe physical . . . maybe emotional. You probably watched her learn very well how to live in an oppressed space. And, although you probably vowed never to walk out a life in such a hurt space, here you are . . .

You see, when we journey with our mothers (or others) through their pain, the things of pain are what we learn best. We learn the face of humiliation. We learn the taste of oppression. We learn the acrid scent of self-defeat. When we learn pain better than we learn joy or peace or any of the other good things, pain is what we allow to define us.

At times it may feel almost noble to reassure ourselves that we have been wronged. But it's time for us to know that the difficult times we've gone through do not give us worth or take worth away from us. Emotional pain is a personal possession. And as owner of the pain, we can *choose* to give it up . . . to give it over to some other perspective that will do us better. To create new feelings of lovingkindness out of our pain. Our sad experiences are of the greatest value when we allow them to strengthen us and make us sensitive to the needs and the feelings of others . . . now that is something! Isn't that something?

Arise from the depths of yourself . . .

At times life can become such an unhappy place to be that we can't bear up anymore. A weary brand of sadness attaches itself to our being. We feel depressed. Forced down hard by every little thing we've been trying to handle, trying to do right, trying, trying, trying to control. Depression makes us realize that our life must be re-balanced if we are to ever be glad to be alive again. And today is the day we have to begin because depression says to us that there is no more time. That we are, right now, in danger of imploding, falling down and apart inside ourselves . . . of becoming a walking wound and no longer the vibrant woman we were created to be.

When depression claims us, it can be a blessing. All of the energy that we were using to run full speed in the wrong direction—away from our Highest Self and away from our Greatest Good—is cut off, and we are forced to stop and just *sit*. Our Inner Woman becomes so fed up with the way we've been treating ourselves that she pulls rank: 'Sit down now.'

And you have no choice but to listen to what she has been trying and trying and trying to make you know. Now she can tell you that all this giving and giving and giving pieces of yourself that you've been doing is not good if you are not taking care of yourself. Giving to daughters, giving to sons, giving to jobs, giving to church, giving to husband-lover-mate, giving . . .

Now she's going to tell you what you've been trying not to know: that you DO have limits . . . that you cannot continue to scale mountains and leap rivers if you are not taking sufficient time to sit in God's Spirit and drink and be fed and be nourished and strengthened. If you are not sloughing off the stuff of daily life to be renewed and give thanks. Now your Inner Woman can stop you from going deeper into trouble. As you quiet yourself to listen, your Inner Woman can explain some important things to you.

Now, my Sister, that your Inner Woman—who is, by the way, the one who first hears God's Holy Spirit—has your attention, your healing can begin!

Why? . . .

Walk the low places of our life when High Places are waiting for us?

Why?

Struggle miserably through our days when our spirit is connected to God's powerful Spirit?

Why?

Moan mournful songs when it is already morning and Joy is already here?

Why?

Sit pitiful when our spirits are already dancing . . . already occupying the spaces we want to be in?

Why?

Emerging from dark times . . .

Every woman has dark times during her life.

Sometimes they emerge when we have just gone through some difficult circumstance, such as divorce, or the death of someone we loved, or some other loss or change.

Sometimes we feel powerless to help ourselves to think any better.

Sometimes we can feel ourselves having a most torrid and intense love affair with our personal pain.

If only we will trust our Inner Woman as she works to put the experiences we've walked through into a perspective . . . coming to know that our Inner Woman must bleed our deepest wounds in order to prepare us to be healed . . .

If only we will remember to know that we are not ever alone. That even if our pain is so great it causes a chasm between ourselves and every good belief we ever had, this does not mean that God is not sitting right beside us . . .

If only we will know these things, we will emerge from our walk through the depths of Self, strong and steady. Never the same as we were. But surely, surely better.

Ready? . . .

We swim, daily, in whatever feelings we are having. Stroking, floating, treading steadily through them, we try to go about our lives. And sometimes, if we aren't mindful and prayerful about what's going on inside of us, we can get stuck in some negative spaces and stay there much too long.

What if you were abused, emotionally or physically, as a young child? If you spend your days stuck in the pain of those experiences, you will be abused, continuously, every day of your life for the rest of your life, or until your mind takes drastic (and probably negative) measures to relieve you of this trauma.

What if you had your first child when you were fourteen, and you cannot recover from the shame they made you feel? Will you spend the rest of your life concentrating on finding the best ways to hide yourself? Your dreams will not get much of your attention that way. In fact, by now you may have denied yourself the privilege of ever dreaming again.

What if you didn't finish high school, or college, or the master's program, and now your eyes fill with tears whenever you attend a graduation, and you feel as if everyone in the world knows and thinks you're not smart enough? Will you walk around for the rest of your life feeling like you've cheated yourself, denying your natural desire to learn new things and to accomplish some things . . . working at jobs below your potential and maybe struggling financially?

It's how you handle your pains and disappointments that will determine whether or not you will move toward your High Places. Too often we make our pain our familiar, our favorite preoccupation, our most common and comfortable thing to think about. We carry it around in our minds and wrap it around us like a tattered old security blanket that makes us reek of hopelessness and chokes off every single dream we ever hoped to have.

Get ready . . . to jump over that part of yourself that's attached to this pain. Jump! Cease meditating on your pain and begin to meditate on the path.

The first step . . .

There's no denying it: Life offers us all some pain. But all pain is not the same. And it helps to differentiate between the kind of pain in our life that's caused by circumstances and other people, and the pain that we cause and hold to ourselves.

There is the pain that comes from sitting and staying in a painful space—a puddle of pain—day, after day, after day.

And then there is the pain of change, the pain that comes from losing someone we've loved, someone who supported us, someone we depended on.

The first step out of pain is to acknowledge that the pain-space is not where God chooses for us to stay. This is the first step to becoming emotionally and spiritually whole women.

Meditate on your life:

What Dream, Vision, Idea, Love, Hope can I walk toward to walk forward out of this space?

What new strength has this pain given me?

Is there someone going through some experience similar to my mine that could be comforted if I share my thoughts about my journey?

What thoughts and experiences can I share with my daughter that will help her learn how to walk through pain?

What am I learning that is of value to myself . . . and so to my daughter?

Saving her from saving you . . .

We can never be sure exactly how walking with us through our pain may affect our daughter's life. We have no way of knowing, in advance, how she will internalize her experiences and her perceptions of our experiences. We can be sure, however, that whenever our daughters accompany us through a rough space of life, they are being affected.

If our daughters are constantly feeding off of our negative emotions, our anger and bitterness, they develop a pseudo-hardness in response to that sadness they see in us. They're trying to save themselves and trying to help us save ourselves . . . trying to save us from ourselves . . . trying to save themselves from us. If we don't figure this out, they will have to take our place in the battle.

What can we do? We can talk to them about what they see us going through. And we can make sure they know we understand that they are going through some changes, emotionally, as a result of our experiences. Talking with our daughters as much as we can, as we walk together through whatever, together, gives them a chance to examine and discuss their feelings in the now . . . before these feelings become old baggage for them to carry further into their lives.

Teaching her to love herself . . .

We have to be careful that we don't become the greatest advocates in our daughters' lives for turning them against themselves.

Even more damaging than our ancestors' bout with slavery, even more disparaging than our continuing experiences with racism, even more self-effacing than some of our ego-damaging relationships with men and significant others . . . is our experience of self-abandonment.

Many of us have stepped away from ourselves.

The only way to cease our struggles is to step back into ourselves. What has God's message always been to us? Love, right? And Faith that God will enable us in all the details of our life. So, Love must be our springboard for change—starting with ourselves. If we don't make the conscious effort to come to self-love, there is no going any further on our paths to our High Places. There is no teaching our daughters to be any better than we are. There is no teaching our daughters to do any better than we've been able to do.

The secret of ourselves is locked away in a message of Love. Self-love is the step we must stand on to get to the next, loftier step of loving our daughters loud and strong.

Paying attention to what she is teaching you . . .

Just as a mother can look at her daughter and *know* that she is going through something on the inside, so can daughters just *know* about their mothers. Although there are times when we appreciate this special cognizance even less than our daughters do, as we grow more fully into ourselves and as our daughters grow more fully into themselves, this capacity that we've been gifted with, that allows us to understand, if not agree with, one another becomes invaluably precious.

Mutually, mothers and daughters have a Spirit-given agenda as we relate to each other. As mothers try to teach and guide daughters, preparing them for the myriad states-of-being that womanhood encompasses, strengthening them so that they will be able to stand up within themselves, and lavishing love upon them, so that good love will be familiar to them; daughters, too, come to help mothers develop Self in special ways.

Some of our daughters may be trying to teach us Faith. Some may come teaching Forgiveness. Some were sent to help us find our Joy! Some daughters are here to teach us Patience. Some daughters will help us to know our Strength and Power. Some will show us how to give Real Love to others and ourselves.

Think about your daughter. Think about her obvious, and her subtle, strengths and weaknesses. What has she taught you, already, about yourself? How has she blessed your WomanSpace?

Real healing . . .

How can Love ever be good if the vessels are so fouled and tarnished . . . with so much residue from hurts and sadnesses left in the crevices? How can the love we give our daughters ever be good enough for them to pass on and on and on?

Many of us, when we look at someone less fortunate, less learned, less prosperous, less spiritually-aware than we think we are, have grown fond of saying, "There but for the grace of God, go I . . . " But until we can look at people and say, "There I am . . . ," the real healing can't begin.

Only when we can see ourselves in another person . . . and only when we can feel another person in us . . . can we accept the reality that we were all created in Love by a Loving Creator. This is the starting point for us to be able to forgive ourselves and forgive others.

We can be healed of so much of the pain we feel from bad relationships when we really get it into our knowing that a person can only do what a person knows to do. That a person can only produce a quality of love as good as the quality of loving they've been able to receive.

Then forgiveness comes easier because we are able to, with time and some distance from the experience, love them for who they were at the time . . . the best they could be.

Our Woman-Work is to re-open doors that sad love forced closed. Our Spirit-Work is to rise above our own humanness and do what is not humanly possible—to give up claim to our emotional wounds and begin to walk as if we are greater than ourselves. This is Holiness.

From Fear to Courage

I am afraid . . .

I am afraid
but I'm not really sure of what.
Sometimes, when I think deeply,
I can associate the whispery feelings of fear
with feelings of solid fear
I had in the past.

Long, long ago fears
that have no more logical basis
but are still like heavy rain clouds
. . . threatening.

Unconnected, irrational fear.

It lives in me like it has some right
and some definite reason to be there.
Sometimes it hides.
Sometimes I jump over it and think it's gone . . .
I licked it . . .

but it just jumps out of some other corner,
scaring me into shallow breaths
and that foreboding feeling
. . . threatening.

Feeding her more than your fear . . . .

Sometimes our fear has a face. And sometimes it is the *only* face of ours that our daughters get to see. We hide behind our fears, pretending we don't have hopes, pretending we've stopped dreaming. Pretending we're dead.

What will happen if you unwittingly feed your daughter your fear with her breakfast?

And what if, by mistake, you offer her fearful advice for her relationships?

Who will rescue her if you trip in your Walk and accidentally douse her dreams with your fear?

What if you sleepwalk into her soul-space and plant seeds of fear in every crevice?

And when you look at her and see fear bloom and see yourself . . . won't you cry such bitter tears for all your good intentions?

In times like these . . .

When your daughter has children . . . when she reaches into her MotherSpace to find the Love to give . . . what will she find to feed her babies? Will she find the courage you gave her? Will she find your Peace? Will she find your Confidence and Strength? Will she be able to retrieve a bit of leftover Hope? Oh, how she could use your Patience to get her through some times. It's your Faith that will teach her to cradle sick little ones and not fall prey to panic . . . but fall to prayer.

In times like these . . . and in times like those to come . . . biting the head off of fear with clenched teeth of Faith is the only saving Grace.

I had forgotten . . .

we are still the dark and comely wives of Solomon
and we are still the Light, the breath of God
put into us to sustain us in this world

running through our veins is still
the royal blood of God-breath
and the rich particles of Africa's black earth
still mixes with our blood and makes us deep and dark

I had forgotten I am just learning me
I had forgotten
because it was easiest to forget,
I forgot I am just re-learning me

I used to sit and rock baby queens and kings
I used to twist my hair into sweet ringlets
that sang around my face and made me happy

I used to belong
and so I used to belong to me
I forgot, I had forgotten,
I belong I belong I belong to God

my child, I am so sorry
that I became so steeped in foreign ways
that I forgot how to love you
I am so sorry
that I absorbed so much poison fear
that it seeped into you . . .

Giving her more than protection . . .

It is so hard for us to let our daughters into the vulnerable spaces of our lives because we don't want them to know how raw Real Life can be. My God, how we wish that we could make the world perfect for them. How we wish we could offer them miraculous wisdoms that would carry them from mountain-top experience to mountain-top experience without any slips, or falls, or failures. We want for them the life we envisioned for ourselves.

We worry about how to protect our daughters when the feared thing finally happens: when the divorce is final . . . when the business goes bankrupt . . . when we don't have enough money . . . when our illness has progressed.

But the real problem is not divorce, or financial difficulty, or illness, or any of the other challenges life offers us. We, ourselves, create additional hurdles when we try to hide Real Life. Protecting our daughters from reality by creating false fences of security is not at all to their benefit. Our daughters, too, will experience divorces and bankruptcies, relationships turned sour, miscarriages and illness, and other sad fare of life. They will not be progressing through life in a protective pink bubble of carefreeness. They will come to know, as we do, Real Life. And as they walk with us through our Real Lives, they will be learning how to handle their own fears.

We must come to realize that our best efforts for today, coupled with as much faith as we can muster for today, is *good enough*. It will probably amaze us, in the future, to find that when we thought we were at our worst—failing ourselves and our daughters miserably—the most precious seeds of Strength were being planted.

She needs to know . . .

Have you ever noticed how hungry your daughter seems to be for details about all phases of your life?

Part of your daughter's growth toward her own womanhood involves coming to understand your walk through your womanhood. Perhaps she knows this instinctively. Perhaps that is why she wants to know all about how you came to be the woman that you are, even when the telling may make her—or you—feel uncomfortable.

Your daughter needs to know what has caused you pain. She needs to know how you managed to escape the grip of that pain.

Your daughter needs to know whom you loved and how you loved. She needs to know who broke your heart. And how you recovered.

Your daughter needs to know the reasons for your joy.

Your daughter needs to know what made you fall down inside yourself, and she needs to know what made you stand again.

Your daughter needs to know how you have made an inner space of self-understanding and self-appreciation for yourself, so that she can know to fashion such a space inside herself.

Your daughter needs to meet you soul-face to soul-face. She needs to know you.

The real you . . .

There is so much of you being left untold because of fear. Fear of this, fear of that . . . fear of not knowing . . . fear of not being adequate.

Practice, today, being the real you.

It is time to work on the WomanSpace within yourself. At your center, you are Joy. And Gentleness. And Peace. Go to that place and sit awhile. That place is the Real You. Go there often. Practice, practice, practice being the Real You.

There is a wonderful, wondrous energy that is you. This You-Energy is your spirit. This You-Energy is the life-switch between you and God, and as long as you walk this planet, you are "switched on" . . . linked to the Creator-God's energy. This link is your Love source . . . your Wisdom source . . . your source of Peace, Healing, Knowledge.

From Anger to Forgiveness

When she's angry with you . . .

Many times our daughters get angry, for us, about our relationships. They get angry when they think that we are shortchanging ourselves or when it seems to them that someone is somehow taking advantage of us.

After a time of getting angry *for* us, our daughters may get angry *with* us . . . for not acting in the way they think we should act to protect ourselves, to keep ourselves from repeated harm. For not advancing ourselves along a path they feel we should be taking (or along a path that we have been telling them we wanted to be taking!).

Often their opinions, while full of love and concern for us, are shortsighted because of their lack of real life experience and real life reasoning. But sometimes they are actually seeing the situation more clearly than we are . . . *sans* the excuses we've come to lean on, the fears we've formulated over time to protect our ego, and our laziness when it comes to pushing ourselves out of tired situations and on to a much greater Good.

Sometimes, if we were to listen to the faith our daughters place in us, we might find ourselves walking right out of trouble and getting back on the road to our High Places . . . even times when we didn't realize that we had gotten off . . . walking toward new blessing in our lives.

When you're angry with her . . .

Part of raising daughters is butting heads with them on a regular basis. Many of us have a quiet fear of our young woman-daughters. An unspoken fear of their responses to us, of their being able to see and expose something in us that we've been able to keep secret . . . up till now. We know they know us like no one else knows us. And we fear they will say something about us that we can't bear to hear.

With your daughter, you may begin to feel that you are battling for the same ground you already went to war over with your own mother. And sometimes it can be easy to forget that *you* are now the mother.

You may find yourself getting so caught up in the battle that you forget about all your need to teach her, all the questions inside her needing answers. And you may forget that you are both battling toward the same end: for her to grow up to be a healthy, happy, emotionally-fulfilled woman.

In the heated moment that you both are standing in, you may think an interaction with your daughter is a challenge to your woman-integrity . . . a threat to your authority . . . a thorn in your side.

In the tense moment that you are both standing in, you may think that Daughter-Dear is acting too big for her britches . . . is trying to be too wise for her years . . . is coming dangerously close to disrespecting you . . . is acting too much like a grown woman.

But as you are fully present in the moment that you both are standing in, try ever so hard to look at her and see what it is she's really asking you for . . . what she really needs from you, right now.

Take the time to turn inside yourself and ask what this lesson is really about . . . for both of you.

When you're both hurting . . .

When someone has hurt us, we immediately begin to look for ways to keep ourselves from being hurt again. We cover ourselves with the hardest emotional shell we can create. We adopt a self-consciousness that chokes us on the inside and stops us from doing or saying anything spontaneously. We become so adept at self-censoring and self-evaluating our responses that our words and actions seldom come out true. And so we are no longer Real.

We have all undergone some hurtful experiences. Surely our mothers, our fathers, our friends, our brothers and sisters, our lovers, our mates were not perfect . . . and so they, at times, hurt us. Just as we are not perfect and so we, at times, hurt others. But no matter how great the hurt, how splintering the infraction, it could not do the harm that we do when we close ourselves off from Loving.

Being afraid to be Love is a serious thing. The worst, I think, of all fears.

It may be that the answer to every problem we have involves Forgiveness. It may be that we are responsible for a large measure of our own healing through Forgiveness. Once we make the decision that Forgiveness will be our way, a huge door that we fashioned out of hurting . . . opens! This protective door may have been keeping the painful Love out, but it was also keeping our own good Love in. A fountain of positive energy that Unforgiveness has been holding back is suddenly released and can flow freely through us and from us!

Forgiving her . . .

Right in the middle of mother's anger is a particularly difficult place for a daughter to be. She has to interact with you. She needs things from you. She has to ask you for things. She can only avoid your presence for a short while. Your love and approval and acceptance are so important to her that she feels suffocated when you withhold these nurturances from her. If you persist in withholding, she will be forced to seek love and acceptance from any other source available to fill the void.

It's terribly unfair to refuse to forgive a child. Even when the offense has been great, we cannot hold onto our anger or we will cause serious emotional pain. We, the mothers, have to be the ones to forgive quickly . . . and repeatedly. Our influence in our daughters lives is too great to keep throwing their mistakes in their faces.

Our unforgiveness can stop our daughters from growing.

Forgiving yourself . . .

My God,
I greet you today
honoring my spirit's
connection to You.

I come gratefully
acknowledging
that because You are Love
I can forgive my self.
I can forgive my father.
I can forgive my mother.
I can forgive and forgive.

I forgive myself for not giving all the love I feel inside.
I forgive myself for not trying harder.

I forgive myself for condemning myself.
I forgive myself for not believing in myself.

I forgive myself for not trusting God.
I forgive myself for not reaching Higher.

I forgive myself for not having enough Faith.

Because You are Grace
I can rest
my piece of spirit
in the totality of Your Spirit
and be made whole
and be made ready.

Because You are Strength
I can be strong.

Because You are Peace
I can choose peace in all things,
at all times.

Because You are Wisdom
I can know what to do.

Because You are Joy,
hallelujah!
I can know joy!

Because You are Faithful
the measure of faith that I have
can move me closer
and closer
and closer
to the blessings
in my life.

Real Forgiveness . . .

There is the forgiveness that is as simple as saying "no problem" to a friend who has arrived a little late for your lunch together. There is the forgiveness that you smilingly give to someone dear to you who has forgotten your birthday. Then . . . there is the forgiveness that you try to muster for the one who has betrayed your heart and made you bleed profusely on the inside. Forgiveness for the husband who has made love to another woman. Forgiveness for the sister who has told your most precious secret. Forgiveness for the business partner who squandered what you've worked for. The kind of forgiveness that is not humanly possible because the wound is so deep.

Real forgiveness can only be an act of Spirit. With our minds, we can initiate the pardon, but it is Spirit that must actually work to close the gaping wound. Only Spirit can stop the emotional bleeding and begin the healing process. If you have ever thought that there is a person you could not forgive, perhaps it is because you thought you had to do this Holy Work yourself.

Your *willingness* to forgive is all that is required of you. Your willingness to surrender your pain, to get up out of, and walk away from, the victim seat. Your willingness to tell Spirit, "Okay . . . I have entertained this pain long enough . . . I have pitied myself long enough. I have spent enough of my time going over and over these events and circumstances in my mind. I've learned all I think I can possibly learn, and I'm ready to move on, now."

Our willingness to forgive lets our Spirit know that we are ready to go forward. And we need to understand that until we forgive, we can't go forward. Our willingness is the key to everything.

From Weakness to Strength

She has your weakness . . .

You knew this would happen. You figured it would. Actually you feared it would. Here she is exhibiting you. She has your weakness, and she wears it just as well as you do. The only problem . . . she hasn't yet come to realize that it's a weakness. And the fear she's seen you walk around in for all her life feels as natural to her as the climate she was born in. She uses your relationships to gauge her own, and she treats herself the way she's seen you treating yourself for years. Here she is! Fighting your battles, eating your same brand of humble pie, and making the same excuses you originated. You could close your eyes and stuff your ears so you don't have to go through this again . . . but who would save your grandchildren?

Weakness as a starting point . . .

Somehow, our weaknesses always seem to work themselves back around into our lives, testing to see if we've become strong for real . . . or if we were just puffed up with a little fluff of hope for a moment.

If we hold tight to our weaknesses—refusing to wrestle with them, refusing to use the power of our own Strengths—our dreams can get stuck for years, or decades, and may even eventually die.

If we refuse to become active participants in the lesson-situations presented to us, our visions can become like silly fantasies that play out over and over again in our heads, until we squelch them in anger and frustration and shame.

If we refuse to learn the lessons presented to us, we can stay trapped for years in negative circumstances.

As we look at ourselves to see who we really are, we have to promise ourselves total forgiveness for all that we've done . . . and didn't do. For all that we've said . . . and didn't say. For all that we couldn't know . . . then.

We have to realize that these cracks in our being are actually places where we can concentrate on letting the Light into our lives. A designated starting point for beginning our walk up to our High Places.

From the depths of yourself . . .

From the depths of yourself
it is time to rise.
From the ashes of your latest disappointment
it is time to rise.

Your self has been waiting for
your Voice of God within to love you
Strong again.

Your heart has only been waiting
for your permission to
Love again, for Real.

You have always known,
Your spirit has always known,
the reason for your Strength . . .
the real and only reason
why you haven't cracked by now
into a million or so irreconcilable pieces . . .
the reason for your Strength
is that your spirit was whispering
Hallelujah! all along.

Hallelujah, Hallelujah, Hallelujah
Hallelujah, Hallelujah, Hallelujah
Hallelujah, Hallelujah

While you stood shading your eyes
from the heat of the situations and circumstances,
your spirit has been waiting in the
shadow of God's Almightiness,
in the secret place God made
for waiting and getting healed and
being restored and getting Strong and
sitting in Patience for this day.

This time of coming forth
and being Real.

This revelation time of our
our Purposes, our Causes, and our real Visions
as they came to us through a corridor
straight from the Holy Spirit . . .

God is giving woman back the years
the locusts have eaten
and
none of the weapons formed up against us
shall prosper.

God is washing away the years
of residual sadness
and sorriness and sickness—
healing our hands so that we can heal many.

And
the weapons of our warfare
will not be carnal,
will not be reasonable—
will have to be in love.

There is something about to happen.
Can't you feel that?

And Spirit has said that, to be ready,
all Queens must come up
to the Highest Space of themselves
and get ready to walk
in their Highest of Places.

Dealing with limits . . .

Have you known a woman who succeeded against the odds? A woman who became so focused on an ideal or a vision that, with seemingly superhuman capability, she did the impossible?

Focus is the key. Focusing on the thing you are *doing* instead of focusing on the elements of your inability to do it. Worrying about what you *aren't* and what you *can't* do takes so much energy that it stops who you really are from moving closer to your High Places. And it stops you from ever having the chance to see what your real Strengths are.

Only when you can accept your shortcomings and your own personal limitations can you begin to accept your Strengths. Only full acceptance can set you down in a firm base of reality, grounded and settled enough to go about doing the things you were created to do, with a clarity and singleness of focus unclouded by self-illusion and self-doubt.

You will learn the skills you need to know as you begin walking forward. You will gain the knowledge you need to have in the process of your doing.

Growing strength . . .

Did you know you could grow Strength? Yes, there's a Strength you can grow as sturdy and real as a garden full of collards, close to the ground, bushing out and strong.

You can grow Strength by planting seeds of resolve within yourself. You can grow strong by refusing to bow down to every indeterminate wind that happens to blow your way and leaning hard into the Faith seated deep in yourself.

You can grow Strength and create winds of your own to move you around from field of work to field of work. From purpose to purpose.

When we are faced with new things to do that seem to be beyond all the capability and fortitude we've ever known ourselves to have, we have to remind ourselves that the Strength for every task life demands of us was seeded into us at some earlier time by some earlier experience, just for this time—this day—in our life.

When we find ourselves and our children in a place that represents less than God's best for us, we need to remind ourselves to stop waiting for someone else to do the things that need doing in our life. Or approve of our doing it. We need to open ourselves to what our Inner Woman has been directing us to do.

God always prepares us well for that which we're asked to perform. Leaning into this Wisdom, we will see our seed-Strengths begin to grow as we walk forward, believing this to be so.

Helping her to grow strength . . .

How will you help to grow Strength in your daughter? How will you teach her about the very personal relationship that every woman needs to have with her Creator? How will you stop her from ever thinking that she should abandon herself? How can you teach her about her Holy Space of Forgiveness? What can you say, what can you do to teach her about Wonder? How will she learn about the precious measure of Creativity that God has given to each woman?

How can you teach her about the Wisdom that she can find inside herself when she learns to get still and listen to the voice of her Inner Woman? How can you teach her about sister-friend Love? About man-woman Love? About mother-child Love? About mother-daughter Love? About Love of her visions? The Love of solitude? Love of the things God created? Love of praise and worship?

All that you want your daughter to learn, you must have learned to honor yourself. All that you want your daughter to love, you will have to practice loving in front of her.

All that you want your daughter to know, will she first know it in you?

Your daughter is watching . . .

A daughter's self-image is so tightly entwined with her image of mother that she can sense from a very early age how her mother feels about herself. And she interacts with her mother on the basis of that perception. The daughter of a woman who has truly come to a place of self-understanding and self-love has a wonderful advantage: All she ever needs to try to be is right in front of her in living color.

Don't we all have such long lists of what we want to give our daughters to give them a boost toward living a good life? We make sure they get the education, the dance lessons, the pretty clothes. We teach them manners and religion and moral standards and how to act like a lady.

But there's more we must do: Stand up within ourselves and own our lives. Find the courage to own our feelings. Find out what's in our heart and follow it. Be unabashedly in love with our Creator-God. Treasure our gifts. Respect our intuition. Arrive at a space of genuine gratitude for our life. Wonder at God's creations!

We are the gift of example our daughters have been given, from the beginning of their lives, until now. Think about that.

Introduce her to her power . . .

If you will show and tell and teach your daughter that her self-sufficiency is within her reach—that her Power and her sustenance will come through the honoring of her special gifts from God—you will have blessed her life.

If you will show and tell and teach her that her connection to God is her resource for all that she will ever need, you will have taught her Wisdom.

If you will show and tell and teach her that Power need not be intense or abrupt, arrogant or wild, you will have ushered her into a Peace-filled space.

And she will come to know her Power well.

From Despair to Belief

No one will know but you . . .

When you've silenced Self one time too many . . .
Self proceeds to commit suicide

And you will miss her Joy
You will have to walk without her Peace
You will start stumbling throughout your days
without the Light she was holding.
You will no longer have the benefit of her Wisdom.

You will feel very alone . . .
Without anything Real inside yourself

If you keep ignoring Self

and entitle your life

the Diary of a Sweet Soft Murder . . .

no one will know but you

how much your spirit

really loved to dance.

What if? . . .

Many of us have been roaming around aimlessly in a valley of Despair for a while. We started out full of life, but now we've wrapped ourselves in grave clothes of Despair and Desperation and sat down to accept whatever we perceive life is dumping on us. Hanging out in places that are death to us. Dead of hope, dead of possibilities, dead of emotions, dead of spontaneity, dead of motivation. Dead houses that we've outgrown and ceased to decorate, dead relationships that we keep squeezing ourselves into like a pair of too-small shoes. Dead spaces. Haunting and musty. Dead spaces that keep us acting dead. Dead reasons dragging us through dead seasons of more sorriness and dread.

What if a new home awaits you, but you are acting dead so you can't get up and get to it? What if there's a new special relationship for you just beyond the next horizon, but you're acting dead and dead means numb and so you can't feel it calling to you? What if there's something wonderful you could do today but you've locked yourself away in this peculiar mode of non-being . . . so you miss out? Again. What if there's someone waiting for you . . . needing you? Waiting to come soul-face to soul-face with your Light and your Joy and your Hope? How long are you planning to act dead?

Come back . . .

We do not make the journey to our High Places alone. We must companion our Self. Strange as the words may seem, we need to realize the dichotomy of Self in order to understand the possibility that we can separate from the Self—abandon the Self, as many of us have done.

You knew long, long ago that you were splitting your wholeness. When you could no longer stand to witness your own pain, you undid yourself. You walked away and left the Self God gave you sitting on a rock beside the road to your High Places. And you drifted away. You never said good-bye. You just proceeded to take your leave of her.

And now it is Self that you keep looking for. She waits for you on that High Road still. And you have been trying to figure out how to get there , to your High Places, when she is the only one who can take you there.

You may have left your Self because of fear, or disbelief in God . . . and tried to create another way for yourself. Perhaps you thought the way Self tried to take you was wrong, was beyond your capabilities, was a walk in the wrong direction. But could you have been wrong?

Self had no choice but to let you find out that to stay with your Self, through every experience—being true to Self, no matter how new and how strange the thing calling your heart seems to be—is the only way you can ever get to your Good.

No matter how many times . . .

Have you ever come to a place in your experience when your heart feels numb? A place in your life where you feel hopeless and unable to change anything for the better?

You can see yourself acting toward your low places . . . but you're not able to change your actions. Maybe you're walking the path of least resistance because you have no Strength to do anything else. Maybe you've stopped praying because you're so tired of your same old problem that you figure God is tired of your same old problem. Maybe you think that, since God has taken so long to answer, you must be asking for something that's unattainable. Maybe you think you've been believing too High. Maybe you think you're not deserving, not worth the trouble.

Maybe you worry that you're out of favor with God, that you've run out of chances with God because you have not done all the things you think you should have done.

What you're forgetting is that God's Love for us does not depend on us, at all. God's Love for us begins and ends with God and has nothing to do with our attempts at perfection, or our falls, in the process of our trying to reach our own ideas of perfection.

No matter how we've walked, or how we've fallen, or how many times we've tried or failed to try . . . God's Grace awaits. Grace . . . God's unmerited favor toward us.

Believing low . . .

Sometimes, when we are walking through difficult times, we are drawn into believing that we are pitiful. We start thinking that things might not ever get better for us. We come dangerously close to believing that all the Good we've seen God pouring into other folks' lives just ran out when it was our turn. Nothing Good for us. We start thinking and believing low.

Here we have to stop ourselves from continuing in this trend of thought. Here we have to start talking to ourselves. Reminding ourselves. Encouraging ourselves. Lifting ourselves up from the doldrums of the nonbelievers of Good. Up UP UP to the place where we can hear the Voice of God within telling us that we are not pitiful. We are Queens in the Spirit! We were created in the image of one who creates, so we are creators! We are full of solutions to problems. Our challenges are not our points of downfall but our launching places to catapult us up into our New Heights.

Only when we learn to arrest our low thoughts and focus them Higher will we find ourselves walking Higher. Only when we are willing to take full responsibility for the power of our own thoughts and choose—every day, in every situation, for every circumstance, for every reason—Purpose over self pity will we find ourselves heading for our High Places.

Believing high . . .

Sometimes when something is wrong in our life, there is no other way to make our crooked places straight than to start walking right into the middle of the mess. Stop focusing on all the things that went wrong before now and start looking forward . . . walking forward . . . toward the way that we want things to be.

How often do we stop ourselves from taking steps in the direction of our good because we have this image in our minds of what people walking toward their good look like? Are you stopping yourself from taking a step forward because you're afraid you'll bomb out? Because you think you don't have the right clothes? Because someone might find out that you live in the wrong part of town? Because you doubt your ability to take step C after you have taken steps A and B? How often do we think up reasons why we can't leave trouble and head for our High Places?

Some of us are living in situations so precarious that we're hanging on to our sanity by a thin string of insanity! So, how do you get out of an insane situation? By using insane Faith! Faith that makes no logical sense at all. By believing so High that it makes no sense at all. By believing that what you need will appear because you believe you are doing what God would like to see you doing. By stepping out with foot in mid-air to do the thing that's in your heart to do, that which you've been waiting and wishing and hoping and praying to do . . . one day.

Decide that today you have just run out of excuses not to take the first step toward it. And start believing.

The money you need to do the thing you need to do will come. Believe.

The help you need will come. Believe it.

Start believing that you are not a pitiful child of God waiting for a miracle but a Queen in the Spirit standing up and doing what needs to be done to walk forward, heading for your High Places.

Helping her believe . . .

What will happen if your daughter is fed the broken-mirror glass of her fractured self-image all during her young life . . . and she bleeds on the inside and grows up to be a wounded woman who looks whole on the outside, but is totally disconnected from herself and from her own real beauty on the inside?

What will happen if no one says enough with their mouth or with their eyes or with their actions, "Baby girl you are beautiful, baby girl . . . you are precious . . . baby girl, you are God's gift to my life . . . baby girl . . . God loves you and yes, yes, yes, so do I"?

A part of this woman will be broken.

Tell your daughter about the whole place inside her where God's Spirit is connected to hers. Tell her that here lies the healing for brokenness. Tell her that here Spirit whispers, *"You are mine, and that is your saving grace. I am the Strength in you. You can do all things in me. As you discover the amazing dreams in your heart, believe in them. As you feel a special lovingkindness and mercifulness and caring for others well up inside you, grasp it and enter into it like a garment and wear it like your own skin. As you find your mind forming visions, walk toward them, knowing they are as real as I AM."*

Much grace is given . . .

There is a certain thing God has for women to do: Pray without ceasing . . . pray without ceasing . . . pray without ceasing . . .

Our spirits pray without help from us . . . the cells of our body pray and pray and pray . . .

And the more we do this precious work—the more the tears flow—the easier tears come . . . for a reason. Our tears are love from full hearts that keep expanding and expanding. Our tears are from an overflowing cup of Grace.

Much Grace is given to us, you know. We are the healing hands of God. And we are being called to heal much today.

The season of grace . . .

The Grace of God was well in place long before any of us became mothers, or daughters for that matter. And yet we try to struggle along without it. Living our lives as if God, the Heavenly Parent, figures we are grown now and no longer in need of this precious Love. Just for the record, God has not been withholding Love from us. God's Grace awaits us all. In every thing and in every way God's Grace enables us and makes us beautiful!

There is Grace for the MotherSpace inside us. Grace is the reason for the healing that can take place inside of us, enabling us to find good love to give to our children, even when we have been through so much, even when we stand in the face of trouble.

There is Grace, too, for the WomanSpace inside of us, where lives the Inner Woman, who keeps record of all that we know and have done and can do . . . all the while being fully aware of the woundedness that is at least as old as Eve.

Looking back at times when confusion clouded our hearts, we say, "What could I have been *thinking*?" And the Inner Woman replies (if we are listening), "You were thinking faithlessness and ungratitude . . . fear and other foolishnesses . . . lies against God . . . but, never mind . . . there's Grace."

In all that we tell our daughters, don't we sometimes forget to tell them about Grace? Grace, the sweetest secret of all? Grace, the new season! Grace, the best song!

Inviting her to grace . . .

My Daughter,
come sit with me and meet
the Sweet Spirit of God.

Come and learn of the comfort
that awaits you.

Come and meet the secret parts
of yourself.

Come and know
the secret places of yourself
that only the Spirit of God
can unlock and show you!
Come and meet Grace.

Offering her a spiritual framework . . .

Do you ever have philosophical, spiritually enlightening talks with your daughter? Where instead of just giving an answer to a question or stating a decision, you actually explain your answer or give the reasons behind your decisions? (You may be surprised at the real reasons behind some of your decisions!) In raising our daughters, "Do as I say" only gets them halfway to where they need to go. If we explain our reasons—talk about our experiences and the spiritual beliefs that comprise the framework that we walk our lives around—we help them to build a workable system of belief for themselves.

There are certain principles that a daughter must be introduced to and become familiar with if she is to know them and master them in her life: Diligence. Stick-to-it-tiveness. Patience. Endurance. Humility. Courage. Boldness. Faith. All of these have a place in her youth-life if she is to grow well and develop into her greatest potential.

Mother must pass her wisdom about spiritual things on to her daughter, teaching her that the Voice of God—which her feminine spirit embodies and personifies—is what will lead her to her High Places.

Teach her that getting through her low places is not the task. That she cannot get to her High Places by mastering the navigation of her low places. Teach her that she will begin her walk to her High Places as soon as she decides to listen to the Voice of God within her. Teach her that her High Places is not an earned position, it is God's Grace for her because God loves her. Tell her, and tell her again, that to walk on to her High Places, she has only to surrender to the Sweet Spirit inside her.

To every daughter . . .

Don't you know . . . ? All you ever need to be a woman with a sparkle in your eye is to remember that the same God who created the twinkling masses of whatever way up in the heavens put that same twinkle down here on earth to be seen in you!

It's time for you to know that, just as God's waters obediently roam and gather, feed and nurture, empower, change and trickle comfort, answering the call of the Creator . . . so must you, through the spirit tide in you, answer God's call.

Soaring through the air with the Wisdom of every flying thing, your spirit wants to navigate the path to your High Places. And come back again and again . . . each time returning to gather more of God's Spirit, and more and more and more . . .

How could your marvelous God have made you anything else but marvelous?

From Trouble to Possibility

Understanding trouble . . .

Trouble is not the sick baby.

Trouble is the mother who won't pray.

Trouble is not the lack of money to pay the bills.

Trouble is the part of you that's afraid to reach anymore.

Trouble is not the attitudes of others stacked against you, or the hand of the one who hit your face, or the infidelity of the husband or the betrayal of the friend, the death of your mother or father or child.

Trouble is the hole in yourself you keep crouching in, preventing the Spirit of God from filling you up and making you whole.

Trouble is a place of no reason. No way. No understanding. No hope. No help. No giving or receiving. A determination to stay in a sad and sorry place.

It takes a good deal of resolve and grit to stay in trouble.

Walking out of trouble . . .

We can stay in trouble an awfully long time. Weeks can turn into years and decades, stalling us in relationships we know aren't good for us and situations that are low places to us.

Many times, the work—the prayer and the mind fixing, the physical planning and the actual doing—that has to be done to take us from troubled grounds to our High Places is work that has to be done alone.

Many times, we will begin to become acutely aware of certain people around us who seem to be purposely planted against our progress.

There are times when we must spiritually remove obstacles. The person, the poverty, the lion, the tiger may be sitting right in front of us, baring its teeth, blocking the Light we're trying to bring in. And we have to deal with it. With prayers instead of words. With prayers, while we act in the direction we need to go. With prayers and wisdom-seeking and meditation and active faith. Walking through reality, armed with spiritual weapons.

Sometimes walking with the Spirit is the only safe way to walk.

Leaving some things behind . . .

As you choose to walk up out of trouble and head for your High Places, you will need to leave some things behind. You cannot carry the heavy ballast of your past disappointments, your past angers and bitternesses, your past fears and insecurities with you. You will need to wash yourself of these and cease giving them your energy. You will need all of your energy for the new things God has planned for you.

Even in the spiritual uterus—in the spiritual growth process—God has us doing these amazing things: Growing ears to hear with and eyes to see with and hands to hold on with and a heart to hold onto others with.

New life won't come easy. If you've ever given birth, you *must* remember: Birth is not neat. Remember? None of the pain was organized right. Nothing could have made it feel right and unobtrusive to you . . . and yet new life arrived. Right?

When you pack up your mind and decide to leave many of your old ways behind, determined to leave trouble, know this: Even in the lengthy process, while we are becoming our Real Selves, we are awesomely in the order of God's way. And frightened as we are . . . we will get there. Hallelujah!

Holding onto your knowing . . .

Sometimes systems fail in our lives. Our plans collapse. Support systems falter. Circumstances that we thought would always be permanent suddenly quake and fall apart, and we're left standing in a dust-cloud of new responsibilities in an uncertain future. Somewhere up above, the clouds of change are moving into a formation unfamiliar to us.

And, inside yourself, you know uncertainty better than you know anything else. You keep changing your mind. And some days you just want more than anything for things to go back to being exactly like they were. Familiar. No matter how painful "familiar" was/is. But at the same time you know that what was good, what once worked, no longer exists. It has been shattered, and either something new has to grow in its place or you will have to move on.

You could stand there for the rest of your life pretending that what is familiar is good enough.

You could pass the rest of your life in an incomprehensible fog of what you are to be about.

You could take two steps forward and two steps backward and one step forward and one step backward and do this shuffle, indefinitely, pretending you are moving someplace, and never ever get away from the spot of indecision where you now stand.

You could tell everyone you know about your grand plans and then you could make up noble excuses for not following through, and you could be right right right in your own eyes. And you could be right right right in their eyes, too, but your spirit would have to cry for you because you wouldn't be trusting her to take you where you need to go. Your spirit would be crying because of all the dreams you sent to wasteland.

Have you ever caught your spirit dancing, pirouetting outside your body, threading the air with her presence, in rhythm with a silent song so Peaceful you cried to be made of something so beautiful? Have you ever cried to know such a spirit as beautiful as yours? Have you ever cried to be in the midst of your gift of life?

Well, if you're careful to hold onto your spirit's knowing that this—all of this life—is for the Love of God, you would find yourself on the verge of an understanding of how powerful you are because you are spirit. How strong you are because you are spirit. How capable you are because you are spirit. How on time and on purpose you are because you are spirit. And how much a part of the Glory of God you are.

Coming back to yourself . . .

We often wind up in a space of trouble when we keep trying to override our feelings with contradicting actions.

Of course, we cannot act on every feeling that we have. That wouldn't be wise. Or sensible. But we do have to come to a place of owning our feelings. When we don't take responsibility for what we are going through emotionally, when we don't make conscious decisions for action . . . or non-action, we create messes that wind up creating confusion and pain in our lives and in the lives of our significant others.

If we believe in Truth and want Truth from others, but we are afraid of any of the Truths in our own lives, we are living at crossed purposes, negating our own beliefs, contradicting our own good intentions.

Do not try to fool yourself. The time will come when you will have to be true to yourself. Perhaps you will come back to Self, crawling on weak knees, with a confused mind and a heavy heart. But, you will eventually have to come back to yourself and to the purposes that God created you for.

2

Befriending your Inner Woman . . .

Taking positive steps out of our low situations can be hard. Feelings of hopelessness, frustration, and mind-numbing fear can color every possible solution impossible. On the day when you wake up and suddenly feel the weight of understanding that taking your life where you want it to go is *your* responsibility—not anyone else's—you may, at first, want to run away from yourself. You may want to get out of yourself, get out of this life you're in. You may want to be someone else . . . or maybe no one at all.

So many of us, upon finally arriving at this space of awareness, find ourselves to be way out in left field somewhere. Way off the path of our True Life and far away from being our True Self. We have ignored, for too long, our precious Inner Woman and tried to be what some external voice has said we should try to be. Until we learn to befriend our Inner Woman and to seek permission, approval, acceptance from this inner voice of Self, we will always be looking outside of ourselves for permission to be, to do, to win, to fail.

Our daughters look to us for the same validation. Your daughter will, as you probably did, go through some changes as she grows into herself. She will think she is not pretty enough, not smart enough, not rich enough, not big enough, not small enough . . . you get the picture. We all seem to think that we're not enough something. But hearing your voice over and over again in her mind . . . telling her that whatever she is or is not, she is enough . . . will push her right along to the place she needs to arrive at: able to believe in herself enough to give herself permission to be.

Introducing your daughter to herself . . .

Giving our daughters everything they want will not make them Queens, heading for their own High Places. Spending hundreds on hairdos and fake nails, name-brand clothes and every popular CD, will not put them in a Queenly state of mind.

Introduce her to herself. Encourage her to create something on her own—a hairstyle, a poem, a recipe, a drawing, some music. Talk to her about her spiritual being, remind her that she is Divine. Help her to find what she needs to soothe her spirit when life hits hard—a long walk, music, quiet meditation, a talk with a friend.

Share your self and your woman knowledge with her. The more she can know about her precious emotions, the importance of believing in her visions and dreams, and the process of creating, first, inside, those things that she wants to have in her outer environment, the more she will value her Self and the gift of her life.

Teaching her to expect more than trouble . . .

When daughters grow up in trouble, trouble is what they learn to expect. The trouble notions of hopelessness and helplessness are more real to them than anything else. They come to think that Good is an illusion. They come to believe that life is a purposeless meander through trials and hardships and, if they're lucky, the occasional good time. They lose the sense that they were born with, that tells them that life is a privileged journey, fraught with discoveries and wonderings about the Glory of God. They completely miss the point of the journey.

No matter what is going on in your life, right now . . . no matter what your past looks like . . . you can refuse to walk yourself and your daughter any further into trouble.

Yes, trials will come and, yes, things will go wrong, but when you choose to walk through trouble toward your High Places, you will find yourself showing her Hope not helplessness, Power not pity, Lovingkindness not a need to destroy others, Wisdom not panic, Faith not fear.

Your daughter will come to recognize that each experience has value as a stepping stone, carrying her closer to her Good.

Stepping out . . .

We are stepping out of our heartbreaks
stomping out of our fears
and our disappointments
catapulting up from our depressions
shooting out of our troubles.

We are coming out of our laundry rooms
and from behind the wheels of our cars
and from our computers
and from our busy-nesses.

We are jumping over the murky rivers of doubt
scaling mountains
climbing trees to see
clearly . . . us . . . the beloved of God.

We are climbing ropes of silvery pure spirit
We are loving loud and strong
We are ready, awesomely ready,
to be who we really are.

From Busyness to Balance

Woman-Work . . .

The realities of parenting may demand that we run around in often illogical patterns to get all the mothering work done.

And the realities of economics may demand that we juggle mothering with jobs, with school, with marriages, with charity work; or mothering with two jobs, a special friend, and church obligations . . . or any combination of the above, depending on where we are in our lives and what's being required of us at the time.

The dilemma of every woman is how to buy the bread she loves to feed her people. How to create the resources to provide the necessities and the comforts she loves to give. How to be effective in the hard copy of life so that the soft calls of her spirit can be answered.

We have come to a potentially dangerous space of existence. If we aren't paying attention, "work," the world, our relationships—and especially our busynesses—will block out the input of the Spirit.

While the necessity of meeting family and economic demands calls us, we cannot forget our Woman-Work. Our study of life. The creating of our home spaces.

The balance we need for our lives will come when we take the time to look within for our answers. If we listen to Spirit, a workable solution will emerge from the mass of confusing messages and obligatory calls. A comfortable rhythm of work . . . give . . . ponder . . . rest . . . will arise if we are willing to be flexible.

It's hard to grow . . .

Yes . . . it's hard to grow when the children need attention, baths, help with their studies, dinner, lunch money, a red shirt for the school program, Christmas, a new computer, a clarinet, a dance class, a pair of cleats . . . and some discipline. For this week.

And, yes . . . it's hard to grow when the man in your life is trying to get your attention, your submission, your cleverness, your sexiness, your time, a pick-up from work, dinner, your opinion of this movie, and his laundry done, please. For tonight.

But . . . growth is how you will get to your High Places. So when your Inner Woman, who is in charge of growth, asks for just a little of your attention . . . just a bit of your time . . . for you to slow down and get still sometime soon . . . consider, won't you, penciling her into your schedule?

Clearing space . . .

Most women know about clearing spaces.

Just as we would have to clear a path, or a piece of ground to plant a garden or build a home, we have to clear a space on the foundation of our life to bring about those things we want to see happen in our lives—and in our daughter's lives. Chop down the weed thoughts that have grown so high they block out the Light. Uproot those unwieldy vines of fear that entangle our feet so we can't move forward.

Clear time in your days. Clear spaces in your home. Clear room in your head for your dreams to start to bloom.

You will need to ask yourself:

How can I change the ways I am using my time to make time for the things I say I want to start doing?

How can I change the ways I now use my energy to make sure that I don't fizzle out before I get to my real tasks?

How can I preserve or create enough resources to enable me to have what I need to support these new goals?

What must I change about these changeable things in order to do the things that I most want to do?

Do I really see myself as a woman capable of doing the things I most want to do?

What self-perceptions must I change in order to become who I really am?

Paying attention to spiritual tides . . .

There are cycles of time when your energies are outgoing, when giving to others, being of service to others, feels right to you.

There will be other times when your outgoing energy wanes. You may notice that you feel fatigued by your normal activities. You are probably ignoring your Inner Woman, not listening as she tries to slow you down and prepare you for guidance about your life. If you were to tune into your Self, you would be surprised to learn that some inner conversation has already begun inside you . . . and your Inner Woman has been trying to get your attention.

'This is something you should hear,' she is saying. 'These are things that you should know.'

You need to start knowing that your Inner Woman will not call for your attention unless it is important. You can only ignore the emotional goings on inside you for so long until she begins to rebel against your negligence.

Just as there is ebb and flow in our physical bodies, we must pay attention to the spiritual tides of our Inner Woman. When she is wanting to slow down, it is for a reason, and we must honor our spirits by finding a way to oblige. Recognize that the Inner Woman is far more in tune with God's voice than we are.

We are at our most powerful and most effective when we follow the gentle stirrings of our spirit. She will never lead us wrong.

Waiting . . .

One of the characteristics the feminine spirit demands that we develop is Patience. Waiting. Being quiet and still in the Spirit—even as we go about our life-work—is required of us.

We waited long to give birth . . . or so it seemed.

We waited long to become women . . . or so it seemed.

Each day awakes with its own urgencies. And still each day our spirits must teach us to pause, to ponder and to wait, again.

Listening . . .

Close your eyes and your mouth and listen to the silent tones of spirit rushing in and around all of creation. Hear the miracle of your heart beating inside you. Now, do you think God created you to be sad and sorry? No!

Listen . . . to the miracle of your own voice speaking in your head. Do you think God really created you to have powerless, unfruitful thoughts?

Listen now . . . what you hear is your connection to all that is now living and to all that has ever lived.

All of the women who have ever lived have had thoughts like yours. Isn't that miraculous?

And all of the women who have ever lived have had thoughts different from yours. Isn't this, too, miraculous?

Being at peace . . .

There is a part of us that has learned to think we can be at peace only when everything in our life is exactly as it should be. Which is, of course, just about never. But we really should start loving ourselves enough to know this: Peace is not something to be attained at the end of finally getting your bills paid . . . for this month. Or on the last day of the course you're taking in school. Or when your daughter graduates. Or when the pregnancy test (yours or your daughter's) reads negative. Peace is not something to be attained only in the face of the temporary absence of trouble. Peace is what we need to walk with through our today-life, and everyday-life.

Peace is our gift from God. A gift that goes along with walking out our days in this human body. Your Inner Woman knows all about Peace. She remembers that God gave you Peace at the beginning of your life. From your first breath, the Peace of God that surpasses our understanding was, and still is, a most precious blessing.

Daughter-Work . . .

Just as we are trying to forge a life-path to follow that makes sense, that gives us some happiness, that stabilizes us, that satisfies us emotionally and spiritually . . . so are our daughters, only with much less wit, experience and wisdom.

If there is one thing we can do for our daughters that will have the most influence, it is to pull them closer to us. Physically, emotionally, and spiritually. Spend more time with them. Look into their eyes. Touch them. Smile at them. Share a laugh. Share your beliefs with them. Work with them. Play with them. Party with them. Worship with them.

How can we possibly know what is going through our daughters' minds if we aren't taking the time to look into their eyes on a regular basis?

How will we know if they know how to love if we can't find the time to give them our good love?

How can we ever expect them to obey us if we have not put in the time and continuity required to establish ourselves in the position of parental authority?

Somewhere between work and housework, home-work and extracurricular activities, meetings and mall-mania, we have got to schedule in time when we are still . . . and totally available to our daughters. To stay abreast of what's going on with them. To get a notion of where they are emotionally. To get a glimpse of what they're thinking.

If we don't keep our young daughters close, they won't be able to hear us when the time comes for us to talk to them. We need to be near to them, next to them, while they are young, if we are to know them, to know how to talk with them, to know what brand of loving they will need as they grow older.

Raising her as you raise yourself . . .

There is a woman inside of your daughter who is settled, strong and wise and courageous, loving and at peace with herself, knowing and comfortable in her knowing . . . patiently biding her time. You may not have seen her often, but could that be because you're not quite ready to meet her?

As our daughters grow naturally away from being the jittery little girls that needed us for everything . . . into young women who are learning to recognize and value the voice of their own Inner-Spirit-Woman, learning to find their own gifts of peace within themselves . . . we must also be growing. And we must also be listening to the voice of our Inner-Spirit-Woman, honoring our own gifts of peace. We must go back to marveling at ourselves, loving our feelings, loving special someones, discovering new joys, or we will not know much about the journey our daughters are on. We will not be able to truly guide them, accept them, and encourage them to be themselves, as we want with all of our heart to be able to.

For a young woman, self-discovery can be so wonderful. Unwrapping the gifts God gives over and over again to find a new facet of Self, each time. Sister, can you remember? Can you remember first love? First dream? First vision? First ideal? First romance? First personal creation? First responsibility? First treasure? First sacrifice? First heartbreak? First recovery? First shame? First real forgiving?

While raising our daughters, we need at the same time, to be raising ourselves.

Telling her about the cycle of women . . .

From the pre-menstrual years, to the child-bearing years, to the pre-menopausal years, to the post-menopausal years, we are many women. And during each stage, we are actively becoming another woman. Our life is the metaphor for all of creation, and we can witness ourselves being re-created and re-invented over and over again.

We need to tell our daughters how wonderful it is to be a woman! How a woman's life tends to be cyclical . . . how her physical, emotional, and spiritual strengths will peak and dawn at different stages of her life . . . how her strengths will depend on walking out her days in tune with her body, mind, and spirit . . . how wisdom about the feminine *spirit* gift comes with age and experience, if she is willing to listen . . . how she will move on to new states before she has a chance to become bored with any stage in life or any one set of responsibilities, if she will listen to what her Inner Woman is telling her.

From Mother to Daughter

Growing . . .

Our mothers are the gardens that we grew in.
We absorbed the acidity, the substance of them.

Like flowers that absorb the nutrients in soil,
we absorbed the coloring of their attitudes,
their receptivity to the sunshine,
their tolerance for the heat of life
and the coldness of pain.

What will we do with who we have become?

What will we be to grow our daughters in?

Their daughters, too, will grow in us, you know.

Pass on the ways . . .

The mother-daughter relationship is the core relationship of humankind. Women bear and nurture life so that more bearing and nurturing can take place somewhere into forever.

What could be more sacred than to pass on to our daughters the ways of relating soul-face to soul-face. Pass on the ways of relaying love. Pass on the ways of relaying spiritual knowledge. Pass on the ways of relaying the means of surviving . . . so that the love can be good and the Spirit can keep on being heard . . . and the loving can keep on making us whole and the Spirit can be heard?

What could be more sacred?

Remember your passion . . .

The gifts of God to the feminine spirit are many. One of the greatest gifts may be our creativity. It seems that we were born with a desire to create a good world for our families and ourselves. If we are not too tired, we feel a great passion toward nurturing.

How easy it is to get sidetracked by the day-to-day fare of life. To forget the special plans we once had in our hearts for our children and for ourselves. To allow our creativity to stay hidden behind pockets of fear. To silence our hearts about the possibilities of good to come. To get caught up in the struggle. To come to a place of possible defeat by circumstances. To forget the things for which we once felt passion.

Today, remember the things that made you know passion.

Remember the dreams you had for your daughter before she was born? Remember the plans you made for her life on the day she was born? Remember the joy you felt about her new life? Remember how she jump-started your heart and made you believe, made you vow that you'd find a way, make a way, for her Good, and yours, to happen?

Grasp that same passion now. It's still there waiting because Spirit has kept it safe for you. Take that thread of golden passion and begin to weave it all through your life . . . and your daughter's life.

Recognize your gifts . . .

Our daughters need to be taught early to honor their gifts. They will learn this best if they can see us giving a place of honor to our own precious gifts. We may have forgotten about that "special gift" that God bestowed upon us to remind us, and others, that we are Queens in the Spirit. We may have forgotten that the "special thing" God enables us to do is our vehicle for going out to bless others.

Today, take a moment to thank God for your gifts.

Does the Spirit sing through you in a voice of resonance and clarity? Well then, your voice is your special gift, and it can help someone's pain.

Were you born with an inner Peace that seldom fails you? Then, your gentleness and calmness and quiet steadfastness is your perfect gift . . . and it can calm and strengthen those around you.

Do you know Joy? Not a joy given of this world, but divine Joy? Or do you know Faith best? A Faith so crazy that sometimes you look at your self and say, "Girl, please!"?

Have you ever seen yourself Light up a room full of sad people who seemed to be waiting for you to come and show them the way to somewhere important? Well, your kind of Light is straight from the Spirit!

Today, promise yourself to recognize your gifts and to offer them every chance you get. Walk strong, knowing that you are well-prepared to do all that you are here to do.

Walk in your beauty . . .

Peace and Grace and Faith on our faces and in our posture and in our walk are what make a woman beautiful, not surface looks or age, or stature or race. When women have beautiful ways, they glow and shine with the Glory of God.

Look at yourself in a mirror and find your beauty. Where does your inner beauty shine through? From your eyes? Your smile? From your hands? Or your feet? You will see that every part of you that you use to relate to others holds your beauty.

Look at yourself with your mind's eye. Where is your inner beauty? Is it in your Hope? Your exuberance? Your Faith? Your Love? Your Joy?

Today, know that you are indeed beautiful!

Celebrate your daughter's beauty . . .

There are messages the Inner Child needs to hear from the very beginning. Positive messages on which to build a strong foundation:

"You are a cherished and valued Creation of God. You were created in Love. You are God's planned-and-meditated-on Creation. You are filled with God's Divine Spirit and so you are Divine, a Royal being, filled with Lovingkindness to give out, and Joy and Light and Peace. You are worthwhile and familiar to God, your Creator. And you are worth much to others here on earth."

Isn't it amazing that if you have someone in your life telling you that you ARE good and precious and beautiful, you really BELIEVE that you are good and precious and beautiful? So many of our precious daughters will never know their own worth because no one will tell them.

The world will tell them many other things. The world will say that to be beautiful, you have to look a certain way. To be powerful, you have to do a certain thing. To be intelligent, you must think a certain way. To be successful, you must follow a certain formula.

The world will never tell them about their own particular brand of beauty. Their own particular kind of strength. Their own unique measure of power. The world will never tell them these things . . . so we will have to.

Believe she will find her way . . .

Watching from the MotherSpace can be so difficult. As we watch our daughter growing up, we become familiar with all the facets of her personality. We get to meet many of the women that she will grow to be. We get to know certain traits of her personality well. We can almost pinpoint exactly what her trials and problems will be later in her life. And we may fear for her.

In spite of our knowing what we think we know, we must believe that our daughters will surely find the way to the Highest End of themselves. We can be most helpful by being willing to let our daughters grow at their own pace, with us supporting them, praying for them, encouraging them, as they need it.

Insisting, for example, that a quiet young woman become more extroverted, or that a gregarious young woman become a mouse, won't help their growth and development one bit.

However your daughter is, today, is how God intends for her to be today.

In time, she may very well progress into another facet of herself, as like unto another side of the same sparkling diamond. But the decisions and the reasons must be hers.

She will find her way.

Help her believe in herself . . .

Much of a daughter's confidence is infused directly from how much confidence her mother has in her.

We might be surprised to know how much our opinions of our daughters matter to them. But think back. Can you remember a time, long ago, when the person you wanted to please more than anyone else on earth was your mother? It is as if every kindergarten picture, every dance recital, every lesson learned, every task accomplished by a daughter is done so she can show it to her mother. And every failure makes her feel as if she has disappointed her mother.

We can help our daughters build good self-concepts by pointing out their strengths every chance we get. There's no need to stress their weaknesses. They'll figure those out on their own. We can help them learn to value Self by supporting them in all of their youthful goals and visions, whether we think they are very important or not.

So your daughter wants to be a poet . . . offer to read her stuff. Buy her pretty colored pens and fancy writing books. If she wants to learn to play violin . . . find her a class, an affordable instrument, and cheer her on.

Providing good opportunities for your daughter to be who she wants to be has less to do with what you can afford or provide, and more to do with what you have faith for and what encouragement love can dig up.

Show her more than your woundedness . . .

When our daughters do not listen to us, it may be because they see us betraying ourselves. When our daughters do not follow our guidance, it may be because they smell our fear and know our confusion. They see us walking further into problems as we seek solutions.

So many of them are having babies young because they want their own good families to love. But they lack the knowing to listen for the Voice of God within, and so they end up confused and at wit's end. They follow whatever. They will continue to follow whatever unless we go and grab them and hold them and tell them about the Grace of God that has for all the years before now healed the woundedness of women.

Whom do you think will have to pray our daughters toward their healing? Who knows better than we do how sad and afraid they really are?

They know our wounds . . . but do they know how we overcame and why we still know Joy? Faith comes by hearing . . . and so does Joy and Peace . . . Courage, Boldness, Light, and Strength.

They have to hear our spirits talk if they are to know.

We have to tell them.

Teach her self-esteem . . .

Many of our daughters are so confused: They think they have to prove their worth and make up their own beauty and come up with a super-cool persona and choreograph a new sashay in order to get to their Good. And they keep wondering why they keep failing. Is it any wonder that so many of them burn out so young?

Teaching our daughters to esteem Self, as if Self were self-created, blocks them from seeking God's intervention in their life and tricks them into dishonoring the only part of themselves that can lead them to their highest Good. Trying to teach our daughters to think highly of themselves without first teaching them the humility that walks hand-in-hand with the precious Grace of God is not wise.

A true love of Self comes when we stop focusing on Self and begin concentrating, instead, on the true nature of the One who made us. When we are able to view ourselves as precious creations in the eyes of God, we become precious. When we can see ourselves as evolving in a process of development that God has authored, we are able to be all right with our mistakes and mis-steps. We come to feel more gratitude than glory for our victories.

When we teach our daughters to see themselves as exquisite creatures, precious because of the Spirit placed so carefully in them . . . teach them to be conscious of their Queen-hood . . . they will walk blessed, knowing they are significant in the vastness of God's Spirit.

Help her sing her own song . . .

As we work to help our daughters grow toward their Highest Selves, we must always keep in mind—and teach them—that one of the most important things a woman can master is how to live in harmony with her Self.

Beyond the value of any system of knowledge your daughter will learn through formal education, or any wisdom she may learn from your experiences, a personal understanding and acceptance of how her own Self works will allow her to approach life with the wonderful confidence that she is *exactly* as she should be. That her shortcomings are as much a part of her design as the seed-strengths she is beginning to notice in herself.

The more your daughter learns about herself, the more balanced her view of Self will be, and the more she will be able to withstand the ups and downs of life as they unfold.

Teach her that the strength of a woman lies in her self-realization. And self-appreciation. And self-love. Tell her, "You have to love your hair. You have to love the way your skin smells. You have to love being with just YOU sometimes. You have to be in awe of the job God did in creating you. You have to be interested in finding out what God has in mind for your life."

Sing to her the song of a woman's life: "Come back to your Self. Close your eyes so you can see what's really real. God and God's creation. Love and living Love. Faith as the major vehicle. Hope as daylight. Peace as the sun. Run back into your own head and through your own heart, back, back to your beginning. You were and still are a part of God's Spirit."

Love her loud and strong . . .

Mother, love this daughter
like a tree loves its branches
and gives them her strengths.
Like the sun loves and gives her light to the moon.
Like the rain loves
and satisfies each thirsty petal of a rose.
Like our God must surely love us.

Mother, bear up this daughter
like the floor of the ocean supports her moving waters.
Like the womb embraces, pushing forth a new life.

And know that she will grow in you. She will grow in the love that you're allowing yourself to give . . . and in the pain that you hold on to. She will learn all you know. She will, at first, assume the attitude of your attitudes. She will smell of your forgivenesses and your holdings. She will smile for your reasons, she will cry for your reasons. The song she'll sing will probably echo the one that's been etched in your heart.

You see, you are her starting place and her growing place, her enabling place and her opening place, her moving-forth-from place. And if you will come to sing your most-real songs loud enough and clearly enough, she will soon come to know her own voice.

From Sister to Sister

We belong . . .

We belong to an elite group of souls on a serious mission of Mercy and Peace. There is Wisdom among us. In the midst of many counselors, there is Wisdom. We are all, in part, responsible for the health and prosperity of the Collective Black Motherspace.

We are responsible for the enlightenment of one another.

We are responsible for uplifting one another.

We are responsible for educating one another.

We are not to judge one another.

We are not to criticize or destroy one another.

Spirit demands that we look beyond our faults and see our respective needs.

Spirit demands that we become sister-friends and mother-friends and daughter-friends.

Does the collective Black MotherSpace need healing? I think so. As long as any black mothers feel powerless to affect the direction in which their daughters' lives are going . . . . there is healing to be done.

How far? . . .

How far could I have walked without the Love other Queen-women have given me, freely?

How many steps would I have had to forfeit were it not for the support my sister-friend offered?

Where would I be now without the Wisdom of my great-grandmother?

How much harder would I have fallen were it not for God's saving Grace?

How many times have I journeyed an expanse, safe in the Strength of my mother?

How many mother-crystal tears gathered to enable me to swim safely across to another important side?

Could I have recovered from my falls if someone-somewhere wasn't believing in me?

Could I have done such improbable things if they hadn't believed I could do them?

What if my Queen-women had never known they were supposed to be different?

What if they had never listened when God was telling them that the weapons of their warfare would have to be Love?

As we are present in this moment that we are now standing in, surely, surely, there must be gratitude for the Queen-women who were born to defy reason and who raised us to believe God.

As we are the force that's called forth to raise the new daughter-women to know more than we know . . . may the Grace of God upon our heads be enough.

Amen.

The kinship of women . . .

How many women did it take to get you through each pregnancy? Who answered your questions and allayed your fears? Who did you tell about the first kicks in your belly? Who listened to your excitement about getting married? Who walked you through your divorce? Who held your heart together after he broke it? Who made you try for that good job? Who rocked your soul when your mother died? Who made you promise that you would never, ever take another hit?

The pajama parties, the telephone marathons, the mall excursions, the all-night chats . . . these are just the beginning for our daughters.

How could we live without our sister-friends, our mother-friends, our daughter friends? Who would understand the depth of our emotion? Who would understand our free-flowing tears but another woman? Who could understand our need to give birth to the new: the new life . . . the new dream . . . the new ideal . . . the new way . . . time and time again during our lives?

Surely each woman friend we have is a gift from God. Surely we wish this sweet solid blessing into the lives of our daughters.

Think now. Can you understand how we women are the hands of God? The huggable, touchable, comforting arms and hands and feet of God?

Start now. Start teaching and telling, humming and singing, this to your daughter: Women are keepers of each other's Joy. We are witnesses to each other's pain. We understand each other's frustrations. We cry each other's tears. We lean against each other's Hope. We dance each other's Joy.

Help your daughters choose Good lives for themselves by making sure they have plenty of positive role models to emulate as they are growing up. The more opportunities they have to get to know Strong, Loving, Capable women who are successfully walking out the lives they have chosen for themselves, the more our daughters will come to realize that they, too, can become Strong, Loving Capable Women who can do anything they choose.

Think gratitude . . .

You were ushered into womanhood with the images of every woman you ever knew. This parade of women gave you woman-images that were seeded into your WomanSpace, images that you either admired or disliked.

The images that were most attractive, most appealing to you were the women that you hoped to become. The opinions you heard voiced about these women became part of your image of them. These opinions were seeded into your consciousness.

The girls we grew up with seeded images into us, too, and helped us to decide, based on our youthful wisdom, whether we would like ourselves or not.

Today, be grateful for all of the women in your life, past and present, who have given you seeds of encouragement to plant within yourself.

And today, release the uncomfortableness that surrounds your memories of those who simply could not know you . . . possibly because they'd never known or loved themselves very well. Let them walk on through your memories blame-free.

Most of all, give thanks for every single woman, from the beginning of your memories until now, who has recognized your soul-face and has shown you hers. For, to a young girl, to have another woman who can see who she *really* is and validate that for her is of utmost importance.

Sister Strength . . .

Think of the women who taught you about Strength. They are the ones to whom everyone runs for help. They are the ones who put out the fires in other people's lives and never seem to have fires in their own. They are the ones who find the bail money. Who feed the hungry and clothe the ragged. They are the ones who gather children for Sunday School and sell chicken dinners to buy new pews for church. They are the ones who nurture the fledgling preachers and negotiate time payments for funerals. And they could care less what you think of them, of their clothes, or their home, or their choice of loves.

Later life has shown you that these women walked like water, changing form when they had to, and always heeding the call of Spirit. Were they born with a special wisdom? Or was there a day when they woke up to themselves and decided they would just be who they apparently came here to be? And then left the handling of the tears to their Inner Woman, who knows that tears are good for grieving lost husbands and wayward children . . . and that there are no solutions to some problems because in some cases the problem is the blessing.

Thank you, Sister Strength, for the ointment that healed, the milk that satisfied, the clothes that kept me warm, the wedding dress, and the burial gown. And, here, for your Inner Woman, is a lace hanky . . . to wipe your eyes. I know, Sister . . . tuck it in your brassiere for one day . . . you don't have time now.

Are you Strength, yet? Are you coming up the long road? To walk on your High Places, you will need to be Strength.

Sister Patience . . .

Have you met Sister Patience. She is so still I thought she was sleeping. But she was praying. You know . . . praying for everybody, everywhere. People she didn't know. People she did. It didn't matter. Prayers run through her like water. Like blood. She sings in the choir, but no one has ever heard her. Her voice is so soft.

She stitches lives together by hand while she's waiting for some things to happen in the Spirit. I bet you thought she was the lazy one. The slow one. Sometimes, she didn't make much sense. While Sister Strength ran around outside, Sister Patience sat in the window, knitting people's hearts together with prayers and planting new seeds of Hope and Peace and things in unlikely places with her mind. I bet you thought she wasn't moving. Wasn't working any changes at all. But if you'll take time to look at her, you'll see she's different every time.

Humming soft songs and, yes, praying without ceasing, Sister Patience walks the Highest of Roads that everybody knows takes longer.

Are you coming? Are you following Patience? Have you learned, yet, that getting there is not the point . . . coming along is the point!

Sister Love . . .

I am God's Lovingkindness. I never do as your reasons dictate. I have only one reason: God's Spirit Loves. If the earth and sun and stars and moon and waters had not already been created, I would have made them for you. Even now, whatever you need, if it is not already made . . . I will make it for you! I am the reason for Grace. Some call me Peace. Some call me Joy. Some call me Light. And , of course, I show forth in all of these. You could call me Sister Love. I will come and answer to whatever need you happen to have.

With me, God satisfies the desire of every living thing.

Sister Joy . . .

I am Sister Joy . . . and nobody has ever told me I smile too much. I'm the song in your heart, the lilt in your voice for no earthly reason. I am pressing back on every difficult situation in your life to help you keep your balance. I am the dance of your spirit, answering the sweet strains of the music of God's call.

Come, see my Glory! Come, taste my free Grace! Come, rest in me, for no reason other than that I AM for you! If you know God, you know me.

Sister Peace . . .

I am Sister Peace. I am who you first were, when you knew who you were in the schema of Creation. I am who you were before you forgot how to be blessed. You just won't be still and so you just can't remember . . . Be still and know that I AM is God . . . Be still and know that I AM is God . . . and you will begin to not worry so. Be still . . . and you will begin to flow through your life like a quiet, winding river . . . doing what you were sent to do and going where you were sent to go. All that is not Peace turns your mind from God into the direction of many nothingnesses. Be still and feel the miracle breath of I AM inside you. Be still and feel your spirit very much alive in the deep of your belly. When you wake up each morning, choose to be Peace. As you walk out each day, choose to be Peace in every situation.

I am a gift to your spirit, directly from the Spirit of God. I am more than enough. More than enough.

Walking into the Future . . .

We are the generation of women who must re-start the living of what we instinctively know.

We are the generation of women who must pay attention so that we can come to know ourselves, and know who we are to God: the Peace-loving, Nurturing hands of God; the Creative, Working hands of God.

We are the generation of mothers who must pay willing attention so the next generation of mothers can know who they are . . . and the next generation and the next generation and the next.

We have to be walking and talking and praying in the Spirit . . . without ceasing . . . or we will not survive. We can all feel this. We are knowing this right now. There is an urgency in the air! There seems to be a silent danger siren sounding that so many of us hear, and we look in each other's faces for confirmation, and we look to each other to be sure that someone else is going through this . . . and that we are not crazy.

But we aren't crazy. In the Spirit there is so much work to do. So much demand for prayer warriors. So much feeding of the spiritually starved to be done. So much teaching and preaching, comforting and pushing along a path. We don't have time to wonder, anymore, whether we are capable. We have to walk, gaining capability. And there is no more time to wonder if our daughters will make it to the highest end of themselves. We have to grab them by the hand and pull them along, no matter how old they are.

The time for planning has passed, and now we are to join the procession of women walking in their knowing to their High Places of Faith. Holy Spirit is shining like the sun and is our Wisdom. Faith is no longer an option but a necessity. The future that has been waiting outside of our world is now in our faces, and the time of allowance for our uncertainty has passed.

We are the generation of women who have to pay attention and listen to what the Spirit of God is saying so that we will know in which direction to begin walking.

Once there was a Queen . . .

Once there was a Queen . . .

A woman sewed for the Queen of the Land from the time she was very young. From the time she was very young she learned to work her days away. The Queen's clothes and, soon, the Queen's daughter's clothes were made of the most beautiful cloth imaginable, rich in color and wonderful to touch. And at the end of every task the sewing-woman asked the Queen if she might have the leftover scraps of fabric to decorate her small cabin with, and the Queen would always say yes. Whatever would she do with scraps anyway? And so the sewing-woman began to decorate her home fancifully with the bits and pieces of color.

In time, the sewing-woman had daughters of her own. And she wanted her daughters to experience the beautiful colors and feel the wonderful textures next to their skin. So, she began to create a quilt, stitching together the crimsons and purples and deep blues and bright golds in a whimsical fashion, adding a bit of flash or color or depth to her daughters' quilt every night . . . all the while talking to them about the things of the world and the wonderful, wonderful creations, the colors and feelings and marvelous things of God. And she never let a day go by without telling her daughters how wonderful they were! What wonderful gifts of God they were! How precious they were! How beautiful and witty and fabulous they were! Each night until they fell asleep, she told her daughters these wonderful things. And when her daughters had gone to sleep, and the night's sewing was finished, the woman lay next to them on the bed they all shared and she prayed for their dreams.

Now when the Queen of the Land had become old, the sewing-woman had grown old also, but differently. The sewing-woman still spent her days working and waiting on the Queen, who had become a miserable, feeble woman. And the Queen's daughters, too, were miserable women.

One day, the Queen of the Land asked the sewing woman, "How? How have you managed to stay so sweet? How do you still stand tall and strong? How are you so beautiful, even though your hair is as gray as mine? How do your daughters walk so gracefully? How is their skin still so clear and their eyes still so bright? Why do they bring such Joy and such Light when they come into a room?"

And the poor sewing-woman, who was not now, nor had she ever been, poor in Spirit, smiled at her mistress, who had scarcely spoken a word to her in the many, many years that she had worked for her. The sewing-woman took the Queen of the Land's hand in both of hers.

"Each morning," she said, "that I wake up on God's earth, I thank God. And the Joy you have seen in my daughters does not come from this world and their Peace does not come from world riches. Joy and Peacefulness are gifts from God. My daughters' Light comes from learning that the more they shine for each other, the brighter they become. My daughters have never been able to depend on anyone else to tell them of their beauty, so I told them and they believed me, and they soon learned to think themselves beautiful. They learned to thank God for every talent given to them, believing their strengths to be their portion—their inheritance from their Creator. They took pride in doing their own Work and they created their own living spaces and they cleaned them. They learned early not to be easily offended. My daughters learned by being and doing and Loving more."

The Queen of the Land began to feel as if life had tricked her and that made her furious . . . but she told the sewing-woman that she was as foolish as foolish could ever be. And she commanded the sewing-woman never to come near her again.

And the Queen of Spirit, and her Queen of Spirit daughters, spent their days Working and Loving each other and Loving their families and knowing Joy and knowing Peace.

And the Queen of the Land, along with her Queen of the Land daughters, came secretly, longingly every day, standing off in the distance to watch those Queens of Spirit walk out their life in their High Places. Wondering. Supposing. What if it really were all that simple?

Photograph by Abdul R. Sulayman. Taken in front of the African American Museum of Philadelphia.

THE DAVIS-THOMPSON FAMILY

ESTHER DAVIS-THOMPSON is an emerging voice in the African American community and a mother of ten children, from the ages of 4 to 23. A graduate of Rutgers University, with a degree in English and a Teaching Certification in Early Childhood Education, she has served as the director of the Camden Free Public Library After School Program and Summer Activities Program. She has also been an instructor at Camden County College in Child Psychology, Basic Writing Skills, and Teaching Children to Write Creatively. As a free-lance writer, she has been published by *Family Circle* magazine. Esther lives in Camden, New Jersey, with her husband, Art, and their ten children, Art Jr., James, Shawn, Patrick, Amanda, Sarah, Colleen, Ryan, Ashley, and Alexander.

Esther Davis-Thompson is available for lectures and workshops. Contact her at:

> MotherLove
> 2443 Denfield Street
> Camden, NJ 08104
>
> e-mail: *edavisthom@aol.com*

© 1997 Felicia Hunt-Taylor

About the Cover Artist

KIMBERLY CAMP, the cover artist for Esther Davis-Thompson's first book, *MotherLove*, has created an original work for the cover of *Raising Up Queens*. The theme of this artwork reflects the importance of ancestors, regeneration, and power for the women in the world.

Kimberly Camp has a distinguished history as an artist, having served as a member of Pennsylvania Council on the Arts, as the director of the Experimental Gallery at the Smithsonian, and as the president of Charles H. Wright Museum of African American History in Detroit. Currently she serves as the Executive Director of the prestigious Barnes Foundation in Philadelphia.

About the Graphics

The illustrations for *Raising Up Queens* were created by INDIRA JOHNSON, Executive Director of the Shanti Foundation for Peace. The Shanti Foundation was established in Chicago in 1993 to foster greater peace between individuals through arts, education, and grass roots community development. Through the medium of art, the Foundation addresses problems of violence, racism, and intolerance that undermine families, communities, and society in general.

Shanti Foundation's art-based education programs help students and the larger community learn that personal strength, creativity, and the ability to examine a problem from many viewpoints are keys to finding peaceful solutions. Nonviolence decision-making skills are interwoven throughout the creation, development, and implementation of all Shanti Foundation's projects.

During the past few years, Shanti Foundation's vision of how to encourage and support peacemaking efforts has focused on child education. "If we want our children to be future peacemakers, we must teach them the skills necessary to problem-solve in nonviolent, creative ways. If we want to diminish violence in our schools and communities, we must teach our children decision-making strategies that result in nonviolent actions."

For more information, contact:

> Shanti Foundation for Peace
> 917 Fowler Avenue
> Evanston, IL 60202
> 847-492-0955 phone
> 847-475-0037 fax
> shanti@dls.net
> www.dls.net/~shanti

If you valued RAISING UP QUEENS, you'll want to read Esther Davis-Thompson's inspiring collection of meditations for mothers.

MotherLove
Reinventing a Good and Blessed Future for Our Children

*"To all of you who are trying to mother
through personal pain,
who are so tired of being tired, I admire you
and earnestly pray for your deliverance
as you continue to daily endeavor
to deliver your children to themselves."*

With these spirit-filled words, Esther Davis-Thompson begins her powerful reflections, calling African American mothers to a "special work." To grow daughters like beautiful sunflowers, worthy and wonderful, with faces full of sun. To grow sons like sturdy oaks with the bendability of willlows, able to catch the wind, withstand, and ride. Each reflection is emphasized with inspiring quotations from people such as Susan Taylor, Toni Morrison, Maya Angelou, Iyanla Vanzant, and Marian Wright Edelman.

INNISFREE PRESS ◆ ISBN 1-880913-38-0 ◆ 160 PGS ◆ 12.00

Spiritual Classics that Call to the Deep Heart's Core

☙ from Innisfree Press ❧

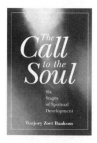

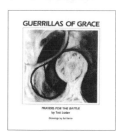